P9-CBB-835

Pebble®
Plus

Meet Desert ANIMALS

LIZARDS

by Rose Davin

CAPSTONE PRESS
a capstone imprint

Pebble Plus is published by Capstone Press,
1710 Roe Crest Drive, North Mankato, Minnesota 56003
www.mycapstone.com

Library of Congress Cataloging-in-Publication Data
Names: Davin, Rose, author.
Title: Lizards / by Rose Davin.
Description: North Mankato, Minnesota : Capstone Press, [2017] | Series: Pebble plus.
  Meet desert animals | Audience: Ages 4–8. | Audience: K to grade 3. | Includes
  bibliographical references and index.
Identifiers: LCCN 2016035496 | ISBN 9781515745990 (library binding) | ISBN
  9781515746065 (pbk.) | ISBN 9781515746249 (eBook PDF)
Subjects: LCSH: Lizards—Juvenile literature.
Classification: LCC QL666.L2 D277 2017 | DDC 597.95—dc23
LC record available at https://lccn.loc.gov/2016035496

Editorial Credits
Marysa Storm and Alesha Sullivan, editors; Kayla Rossow, designer;
Ruth Smith, media researcher; Kathy McColley, production specialist

Photo Credits
Capstone Press: 6; Shutterstock: Alexander Erdbeer, 24, Anatoli Dubkov, 7, Asian Images,
2, 24, Butterfly Hunter, 17, gracious_tiger, cover, back cover, Jason Mintzer, 5, Kharkhan
Oleg, 13, Nick Henn, 19, nj1987, 21, optionm, 22, Photo Love, 9, Svoboda Pavel, 15, Tom
Grundy, 1, Yojik, 11

Note to Parents and Teachers

The Meet Desert Animals set supports national curriculum standards for science
related to life science and ecosystems. This book describes and illustrates lizards. The
images support early readers in understanding the text. The repetition of words and
phrases helps early readers learn new words. This book also introduces early readers
to subject-specific vocabulary words, which are defined in the Glossary section. Early
readers may need assistance to read some words and to use the Table of Contents,
Glossary, Read More, Internet Sites, Critical Thinking Using the Common Core, and
Index sections of the book.

Printed and bound in China.
007872

TABLE OF CONTENTS

DESERT DIGGERS

Lizards dig in the sand.

They hide from the hot desert sun.

Some nap in the sand until

the sun goes down.

Lizards live on every continent except Antarctica. Many live in deserts around the world. They make burrows under bushes or in high cliffs.

where lizards live

FROM HEAD TO TAIL

Lizards are reptiles.

They are cold-blooded.

Their body temperature changes with

the air temperature.

Lizards come in many sizes.

The smallest lizards are less than

1 inch (3 centimeters) long. Large lizards

can be 10 feet (3 meters) long.

monitor lizard

Most lizards have short necks and
a small head. Their skin is dry and scaly.
They have short legs and a long tail.

TIME TO EAT

Some lizards eat buds, leaves, and flowers.

Others eat crickets or beetles.

They catch insects on their long, sticky tongues.

Sometimes they eat other lizards!

LIFE CYCLE

Most female lizards lay eggs once
a year. They dig a hole to hold the eggs.
After that, most mothers leave the eggs alone.

Eggs take about 10 weeks to hatch.

Newly hatched lizards take care of themselves.

They find food and live on their own.

Raptors, snakes, and foxes attack

and eat lizards. Frightened lizards

race to their burrows to stay safe.

Lizards live about 6 years in the wild.

Glossary

burrow—a hole or tunnel in the ground made or used by an animal

cold-blooded—having a body temperature that changes with the surrounding temperature

continent—one of Earth's seven large land masses

desert—an area that is very dry; deserts do not get much rainfall

insect—a small animal with a hard outer shell, six legs, three body sections, and two antennae; most insects have wings

raptor—a bird that kills other animals for food

reptile—a cold-blooded animal that breathes air and has a backbone; most reptiles have scales

scale—a small piece of hard skin that covers a lizard's body

Read More

Bishop, Nic. *Lizards.* New York: Scholastic, 2010.

Brett, Flora. *Get to Know Chameleons.* First Facts. North Mankato, Minn.: Capstone Press, 2015.

Marsh, Laura. *Lizards.* Washington, D.C.: National Geographic Society, 2012.

Internet Sites

FactHound offers a safe, fun way to find Internet sites related to this book. All of the sites on FactHound have been researched by our staff.

Here's all you do:

Visit *www.facthound.com*

Type in this code: 9781515745990

Super-cool stuff!

Check out projects, games and lots more at
www.capstonekids.com

Critical Thinking Using the Common Core

1. What is a burrow? How do lizards use burrows to stay safe? (Key Ideas and Details)

2. How might a lizard warm up if it gets cold? (Integration of Knowledge and Ideas)

Index